GAVE

ALSO BY COLE SWENSEN

POETRY

Landscapes on a Train, Nightboat Books, 2015
Gravesend, University of California Press, 2012
Greensward, Ugly Duckling Presse, 2010
Flare, Yale University Art Gallery, 2009
Ours, University of California Press, 2008
The Glass Age, Alice James Books, 2007
The Book of a Hundred Hands, University of Iowa Press, 2005
Goest, Alice James Books, 2004
Such Rich Hour, University of Iowa Press, 2001
Oh, Apogee Press, 2000
Try, University of Iowa Press, 1999
Noon, Sun & Moon Press, 1997
Numen, Burning Deck Publications, 1995
Park, Floating Island Press, 1991
New Math, William Morrow & Co., 1988
It's Alive She Says, Floating Island Press, 1984

CRITICISM

Noise That Stays Noise: Collected Essays, Poets on Poetry Series,
University of Michigan Press, 2011

G A V E
Cole Swensen

OMNIDAWN PUBLISHING
OAKLAND, CALIFORNIA
2017

Château d'Henri IV, Pierre Gorse (artist) and Becquet (lithographer)
Bibliothèque Patrimoniale Pau / Médiathèque Andrée Labarrère / cote Ee3213.

Collaged photograph by David Le Deodic

Cover text set in Century Gothic
Interior text set in Bell Gothic Std, Century Gothic, Garamond 3 Lt Sd

Cover and Interior Design by Sharon Zetter

Offset printed in the United States
by Edwards Brothers Malloy, Ann Arbor, Michigan
On 55# Glatfelter B18 Antique
Acid Free Archival Quality Recycled Paper

Library of Congress Cataloging-in-Publication Data

Names: Swensen, Cole, 1955- author.
Title: Gave / Cole Swensen.
Description: Oakland, California : Omnidawn Publishing, 2017.
Identifiers: LCCN 2016045488 | ISBN 9781632430373 (pbk. : alk. paper)
Classification: LCC PS3569.W384 A6 2017 | DDC 811/.54--dc23
LC record available at https://lccn.loc.gov/2016045488

Published by Omnidawn Publishing, Oakland, California
www.omnidawn.com   (510) 237-5472   (800) 792-4957
10 9 8 7 6 5 4 3 2 1
ISBN: 978-1-63243-037-3

The Gave de Pau (gahv de poh) is a river in southwest France; in the regional language, the word "gave" means a torrent and is used to designate a major river. Though there are many gaves throughout the area, in the following text, when the word "gave" is used alone, it refers to the Gave de Pau, and in particular, to that stretch of the river that has been historically linked to the city of Pau and the communities immediately surrounding it.

no river rivers / no river knows

                of rivers after / on others wander

on fields is gone / now go

                who goes there / or so

is gone over water

                over flowing / the flower the

fortune of winter / oh so

                over towered / after tower / who is

now the green walking

                on walking / on river

is the river walking inside

                and inside it / it gathers

a herd of / and lowered

                up the plain thing

is combing

                all to a kind thing / is coming

to the edge of / the bank of

                the charge over-reaching

if over a green thing / a bit

                of a sun thing / a thing of the sun

watering none / but the

                now on its own

on a shore owing timely

                a line of sheets out drying

shuffled by wind that still is

                half sun and half them

rivers it widely / widely

                and carry / a river ungainly yet

silvered its handling / its

                call to the ardor, calling it harbor

to see of that river / no

                river / river / no river unseen

river. larger. larger in the sun.

               the river is wide. even farther.

to figure. the surface area of a river.

               a person with a compass

tracing perfect circles.

               it will be a finite number.

ending often. will be measured.

               if ever found the unit.

if ever stilled upon it

               the hand upon it counted:

one river two, two river three

               until new, a bend is turned

and I turned around

               and I looked back down

what looked like time —

               it was the way it moved in the sun

and the way the sun moved it.

The Gave de Pau is a tributary of the Adour, which runs into the Atlantic at Bayonne. One hundred and ten miles long, its source is on the French-Spanish border in a spectacular group of peaks known as the Cirque de Gavarnie.

Nine thousand feet up, the river begins in a 1,450-foot waterfall, then winds down through rugged terrain collecting the waters of the Gèdre, the Gave de Héas, the Bastan, and the Gave de Cauterets along the way. It joins the Gave d'Oloron just above Peyrehorade, after which they are known as the Gaves réunis until they join the Adour seven miles later.

At its height, usually in May, fed by melting snow and rain falling in a catchment area of over 1,000 square miles, its flow averages 4,275 cubic feet a second. The runoff it collects is one of the most abundant in France. And like all major rivers, it importantly contributes to the economic, political, and social dynamics of all the cities, villages, and farms that it passes by and through.

the gave de pau

          river estranged

as it passes below

          the city slow and broad

almost amorphous

          it often wanders sideways

late in the season

          making odd ambulations

deviations

          stretched lazy in the sun.

then wanders off again

          a living thing

slightly lost in august

          if it remembers it.

The moving river:

Throughout the Günz glaciation, which stretched from approximately 1.2 to .7 million years ago, the Gave de Pau flowed through the Valley of Luy de France and Gabas, some 13 miles to the north.

During the next glaciation, the Mindel, covering 700,000 to 350,000 years ago, it moved south and east, into the valley of the Ousse.

And during the most recent glaciation, the Riss, 350,000 to 120,000 years ago, it moved to its present location.

And ever since, itinerant, capricious, reigning over its distances, and from there into their centuries, shifting, and equally capriciously back again.

Over the centuries, this wandering
      has achieved a certain rhythm

      with the river at times returning
finding its way back

      to an earlier path,
a revenant
      as the snow begins to melt

and someone walks along the river in the fog

remembering the river
      rises here
           to keep
coming around a bend in the river
         remembers
         standing at this very spot
where the river turned
      to fog or seemed to rise and float off
several feet above.

rising other / river is a mist

tiny pieces / takes the air

in linked digression / with

silver-edged / to the end of it

in which / too are suspended

between river and sky

was riding by.

suspended wind / in tiny

apart in pieces

links of spider web

ended of it all

are lifted / the difference

hidden in the riding / who

For the past few centuries, this more localized changeability, so appealing in its reckless disregard for geography, cartography, and all other attempts at order, has caused significant problems for land management and city planning, as the river was often used as the boundary between one town or region and another. As such, it might give a town an extra thousand acres one year, only to reassign it somewhere else a few years and a flood or two later.

water water

we please another

all repetition is in some part spell

as all water repeats itself

is answered

carry me over

so over me carried

(all water is over)

bearing a border

we carry it anchor

as it carries us

in a small blue boat

rowed by a large blue dog that cannot look back.

You walk alongside the river. No; you walk always with. Not down, or along, or beside. And you can't help but measure—is it moving faster? And does that mean each molecule of water? Or does a body of water form internal bodies, pockets that move in counterpoint, in back-beat, in eddies? And does the surface ever move? Or is it something underneath that does? Of course, yes, the molecules of water that form the surface must certainly go forward, but does that mean that the surface itself moves too? Then what is a standing wave? What stays? I watch a large branch being carried down by the river, and then a kayaker, moving faster, then turn to walk back upstream like I'm walking into the arms of some thing.

the hand dipped into the river

                    also turned clearer

because it too ran out

                    and in running

           cut

and in cutting

           lost

its further edge

           got farther then

a river doesn't end

           in the sea.

Other books of poetry addressed to the Gave de Pau include:

1835, *Le Gave: poëme en quatre chants*
         by the Baronde Disse.
          "The master of the Trident
                        leaves the sea"

         1958, *Couleur de Gave et de Saison*
      by Louis Ducla.
"Seasons, mad seasons, prodigious of palette"

              and *Sorrom Borrom:*
le rêve du gave, 2010, by Sèrge Javaloyés, "Great
                 tumult,
                 what noise
                 beneath the gaze
                 ot Mont Perdu."

Early industry:

seven there
                    were windmills here
or seven were
                    where the wind had strayed

but it strayed away, and there is no wind here.

and seven other

        woven of water

seven the millrace

        seven the traced

through a filament

        or thread if you will

tie a thread to a tree

        draping the other

end in the water

        the mills turned to flowers

and the flower in its herd

        pulled the tree into the river

through which it made its way.

a windmill. a wash house.

what we could fish out of it.

a living. and something

alive, and there standing

among what we culled.

we dove down in our hands into the

hand in the water.

a hand plows a river, and we list: fish,

power, stone

a city could live off a river alone. a city

alone

on a river could drift

downriver, rolling

stones until they're round.

we found ourselves

on a shore, and on the shore

was a windmill and on

the shore was a wind.

an entire city can be built

of wind, and we did.

The earliest indications of human attempts to intervene in the workings of the river date to the early 13th century. It was the Canal du Moulin, built to connect the Gave with the River Ousse in order to ensure a steady supply of water for the seigniorial mill, built in the lower town, just below the chateau.

Go. Water always, in one way or another, says *go*. And the wheels of it, and the grind within, grounded in, until hundreds of mills filled in the region, a whir in the wind that was taken for wind.

A river is always more than its water; in this case, for instance, *les sal-igues*, the Béarnaise word for the rich flood plains along the banks of the Gave, flourishing with ash, oak, and poplar, a territory used for pasturing cattle, cutting firewood, market gardening, and by birds for nesting and foraging, by moles for tunneling, and by rabbits and feral cats.

riverbank and pasture

                     flock after flock

the willow of the psalter

                     fetter, but faltered, holding

on with an animal hoof

                     as if

the air got sheerer

                     cattle, sheep, goats,

and horses, and they err.

           1375: a woman in the fog
leading fifty sheep to the edge of a cliff, where they all
spent the night, not knowing in which direction the cliff ran.

                   1593: a goatherd
new to the job got lost on his way back, and so decided
to follow the herd, which decided to pace back and forth across the
saligue until morning.

              1711: a man returning after many years away
got lost just a mile or so from his former home and ended up
miles away again, where he spent the rest of his life.

These are but

                    a few examples of
the curve and
                of the turn and of the return
                                            of
                    yet never
even if you were to weave it from the grasses
                                would it encircle
or ever offer
            a figure with a center.

bank and pasture

        the flock another water

1535: a woman asleep

        against one of her sheep

curled tightly into her

        river adorned

a river by nature overflows

        its terms

Most of the houses, barns, outbuildings, boundary walls, roads, gutters, and every other sort of structure throughout the region, are built of flat, rounded stones taken from the bed of the Gave de Pau. They're amazingly uniform, ranging in size from that of a small hand to that of a large hand and in color from light to slate grey. You see them everywhere, as if the river had exceeded itself with perfect precision and the heart of a mason, century upon century of orchestrated flooding carefully positioning each stone.

And thus, the river is everywhere, and everywhere you turn, you
see it
      in its careful
river with its chisel
             one delicate curve or another
and another, an additional
principle
      by which what's added
             is both unpredictable
and inevitable.

And so the river overflowed. In fact, the history of the region is a history of its floods; the most spectacular in the past few centuries include:

1678: At Lestelle, the bridge, two houses, half the church, and the entire cemetery are carried away.

1780: The Bastan and the Gave both flood, causing considerable damage.

1805 (1 Brumaire, year XIV): The Bastan and the Gave both overflow. Damage at Gavarnie, Luz, and Barège.

1826: Flooding of the Gave damages a slaughterhouse, two tanneries, and a mill.

1829: The Gave overflows.

1843: The Gave causes extraordinary flooding from Luz to Pierrefitte; rain and snow until 24 Sept., then warm rain until 31 Dec., aggravated by a south wind.

1854: The Gave overflows; flooding in Grust.

1855: The Gave floods at Pau, damaging the saligue and fields growing hops and flax.

1861: The Gave and the Bastan both overflow; damage at Viella, Vizos, Saligos, Luz, and Chèze.

1862: The Gave overflows; damage to barns and fields around Chèze.

1865: Both the Gave and the Bastan flood; damage at Betpouey and Saligos.

1866: The Gave overflows at Gèdre.

1866: The Gave overflows; damage at Chèze.

1866: The Gave overflows; damage at Gavarnie.

1872: The Gave and the Bastan both flood. Bridges, houses, mills, and roads destroyed, topsoil swept off the fields; severe erosion and landslides at Esquièze-Sère.

1875: Both the Gave and the Baston overflow the entire length of the valley; structures and fields destroyed at Esterre, Grust, Sazos, Saligos, Viey, and Viella.

1880: Torrential rains in the ravines at Sanjou and Sarré wash down debris that block the Gave, causing devastating floods and widespread destruction.

1881: A flood at Gavarnie washes out half a mile of the principal road.

1891: The Gave overflows; damage to a dike at Sassis.

1897: Extensive flooding of the entire valley between the Bastan and the Gave cuts off roads and damages the Barzun hot springs and several houses and bridges.

1899: The Gave overflows.

1901: The Gaves de Pau and de Cauterets and the Neste all overflow.

1902: The Gave overflows at Gavarnie.

1909-10: The Gave overflows, damaging the dike at Sassis.

1912: The Gave overflows, damaging the dike at Sassis.

1937: The Gaves de Pau and de Héas overflow, destruction throughout the valley all the way up to Pierrefitte. Houses destroyed, factories damaged, roads cut off, and dikes washed away.

1952: The Gave overflows at Pau.

1958: The Gave overflows, washing away the bridge at Ayrùes.

1978: The Gave overflows, houses destroyed.

2012: The Gave floods; widespread destruction.

2013: The Gave floods; widespread destruction.

As floods amply show, a river is never alone, but is always part of a network of interactive waters—the Bastan into the Yse, fed by the Gaves de Héas, d'Aspé, de Cauterets, etc. and every stream that was never named and every downspout, all that rain, the Baron de X spitting on the hortensias, there is nothing that is not connected, or as recommended in the Old Testament, it should all be redistributed every seven years.

Floods were traditionally rated by the number of bridges they washed away.

Some bridges:

For the first many centuries of human habitation, the communities that lived along the river were relatively small and poor, and so were their bridges. Built of wood, they washed away with every flood.

1308: Marguerite de Béarn gave the people of Asson the right to use the woodlands and pastures on the banks opposite their town, but she did not give them a bridge.

1335: The town of Lestelle was given similar privileges, and the right to build a bridge in wood or in stone, though not the resources, so whether they ever found the means to do so is not known.

1687: The first stone bridge was built across the Gave at Bétharram. It has survived every flood ever since.

Ditto for the bridge at Coarraze, built in 1746.

1592: A wooden bridge was built spanning the river at Pau and became known as the Pont du Gave.

1734-39: It was replaced by the stone structure of seven arches that, renamed the Pont du 14 juillet after 1789, has become one of the city's iconic images.

March 1, 1814: Lord Wellington wrote in his weekly dispatch to the War Office that the "enemy . . . assembled their army near Orthez on the 25th, having destroyed every bridge the whole length of the river."

Other Ways of Crossing:

Ferries:

1615: A photograph: A ferryman standing
in a low, broad boat early in the evening, rather bored, with the sky
turning purple and the trees on the far shore cut out in black, and he,
too, now cut out, crisp and dark

                              will ferry me over
                  as calmly as ether
as the calmly offered
                  ferry me other

1817: Two women carried away by the current, swept off a ferry that
was temporarily replacing a bridge that had been swept off in a flood.

To ferry is to over
                  as the long flank is to evening
when calmly the water
                              what the calm has to offer
is passing in passing,
                  the light disappearing in its shore.

Or There Were Fords:

Historically, the Gave was seen as very difficult to bridge because everywhere that it isn't a violent torrent running through a gorge, it's too broad, shallow, and changeable. The city of Pau was first established because it was the easiest place to ford the river along a 30-mile stretch between Nay and Orthez. The city seems to have emerged in the 12th century as a small community centered around a fortified structure on an outcropping of rock overlooking the Gave and its ford.

Pau's first great flourishing occurred in the 14th century, when Gaston Phébus turned the fortified structure into a chateau. Then in 1464, it replaced Orthez as the capital of the Béarn.

A lot has happened since, but much of what visually distinguishes the city today occurred in the late 19th century, when the area became a fashionable retreat for the English escaping British winters and taking advantage of the health benefits offered by the thermal baths scattered throughout the Pyrenees.

The Railway Station: 1864
The Cassino and Palais d'Hiver: 1880
The Boulevard des Pyrenees: 1891-99

Horse-drawn omnibuses: 1894
The Parc Beaumont: 1899
The funicular railway: 1904

All are arranged along the top of a butte with a striking view of some 200 miles of the Pyrenees and 81 of its peaks.

By the *Belle Époque*, Pau and its gave had become a visual experience as much as a logistical and commercial one, for nothing is more propitious to good health than a good view.

Views of the Gave:

Anonymous drawing, undated:
The bridge of seven arches

                    lightly sketched

centered, a sharpened pencil

                    lightly in wander

with peaks in the background.

Victor Petit:
The Gave de Pau Seen from the Parc de la Basse-Plante, c. 1850:
The bridge of seven arches

                with chateau rising on the left—we are looking
east, and the Chateau de Bizanos is small in the distance.

And as if they were at the opera, two women, one seated, one standing,
with parasols fashionably angled, and a gentleman several feet behind
them are watching the gripping drama of people and horses crossing a
bridge.

And though this particular view is very common, there are many others:

Pierre Gorse:

The Village of Jurançon, Near Pau, drawing, 1844:
On the other side of the penciled water, a long town runs parallel to the river tossed among its trees beneath its mountains.

At Laroin, Near Pau, pencil sketch, Sept. 23, 1844:
He catches the reflections of trees on the glass water.

The Banks of the Gave at Laroin, pencil sketch, Sept. 23, 1844:
He used white highlights to make the surface of the water solid, and so it mirrors the sky, and so he piled it high with clouds. There is nothing human in sight.

lithograph, untitled, undated:
Again he's used white, this time to create a visual link between light falling on the near side of the river and the façade of the chateau on the hill, which he then triangulates with the white shirts of a group of men working farther east down the far bank.

Victor Petit:

Pau: Pont du Gave, Route des Eaux-Bonnes, 18XX, lithograph:
Now the white picks out the apron of the woman walking toward us across the bridge.

Eugène Ciceri:

Pau: The Chateau Seen from Jurançon, 18XX, lithograph:
And now the white traces the flow of smoke from the train just com-
ing into town, so it must have been done after 1864. The water is
calm; men are piling hay onto a horse-drawn cart. The horse looks
restless, impatient to get on.

Panorama of the Pyrenees, 18XX, lithograph:
The Gave is relatively low and flowing slowly around a series
of small, flat islands. We are standing far off, up on a hillside,
and there are cattle and their people in the middle distance.

you walk along the river

        among the walked along

would river you a mirror

        would the river, too, on—

and too, we are alone.

        you, in walking over

to the shatter or the

        splinter. someone

threw a rock into the water.

        the center of any river is

cut like a crystal

        you could cut yourself on

as you look down through

        refracted facets that fracture

light

        always looks better in pieces.

as does a river, if

        you can split it, if

you can peel it, layer

        by layer and dry each layer

in the sun.

        dry each layer in the sun and

when dry, wrap it around

                    a stone. rivers so

often seem to run, but

                    there's another part of them

that never moves again

                    in their stones.

Charles Mercereau:
The France of Today: Pau's Chateau and its Bridge, 18XX, color
lithograph:

That weather can be made of color alone. The incredible softness of
the air in pale grey-green, in grey-pink, and the complex greys of wa-
ter, sky, and a duck taking off, of a boat pulled up, oars shipped, and
the sky, by now, all over.

Victor Galos (1828-1879): Born and raised in Pau, painted literally dozens of scenes of the Gave, often struggling with other living things: a boy with horses and a cart, trying to ford; washerwomen in winter; a flood submerging a field of trees, but there's a lot of peace in his work as well—sunlight on an open hill; a woman and a cow stopping a moment to look down at a stream from a small stone bridge.

Or I could have sent you a postcard:

c. 1910, Pau: The Railway Bridge:
The river is high in its banks, and the message is written
in the white sky—"The children and I are off to the sea."

Before 1912, Pau: The Oloron Bridge:
Two large, clear cancellation marks hover over the town of Jurançon:
16 April, 6:30 pm.

c. 1915, Pau: The Valley of the Gave:
Once again, the railway bridge is heading off toward Oloron
in a gentle curve.

c. 1910, Pau: View of the Gave:
A lock of the canal takes up the lower left quadrant, with
a man fishing in the lower right and the city of Pau looking
down from on high.

c. 1905, Pau: The Gave and the Pyrenees:
Rather than a photograph, this postcard is a drawing, with
the Gave occupying the entire fore- and middle-grounds,
with two grand houses prominent on the hill across.

c. 1915, Pau: Panorama Including the Gave:
This one's hand-colored in pastel pinks, blues, and yellows
and shows the clear division between the running river
and the relatively still waters of the parallel canal.

And then there are those that feature labor:

A man standing by three cows as they drink from the Gave.

A man and a woman shoveling sand into a cart, the horse's
front feet submerged in the shallows.

Postcards are, by their very nature, anonymous and undated
in the hands that cancelled them.

c. 1903, Pau: Jurançon:
The view is done as an all-around soft-focus dissolve and features
recent industrial growth, including the 330-foot chimney of the new
tramway factory, which was repurposed in 2010 to house the city's
archives, where I am now sitting, writing this line.

And there are hundreds of others in the Mediathèque de Pau's
digital archive, and they all make it quite clear, and the more you see,
the clearer it is, that Pau does not exist without its river and

that, in fact, most pictures of Pau are actually pictures of the Gave with the city figuring as a propitious site from which to view it.

Or you can view it from the middle, on one of those lazy days when the river runs broad and low across the plain between the mountains and Orthez. The water is so clear that you can see to the bottom, down to the stones that built all these houses and roads, and in the middle of the river, a fisherman—it's the opening day of the season—the water coming just up to his knees—casting long and slow downstream.

Where to Find Salmon in the Gave de Pau, by Olivier Dunouau, 1929, himself shown on the last page of the book in a jaunty pose, leaning back, legs crossed. It's the reproduction of a postcard bearing the legend "Oloron: Un Pêcheur de Saumon."

In the book, Dunouau covers everything from the appropriate hooks, flies, rods, and laws (article 5 of the law of 15 April, 1929) to aesthetic concerns—the ghastly tramways near Jurançon and the cacophonous train that pulls in too close to the river at the Pont d'Espagne, frightening the fish, as opposed to those five miles between Billière and Lescar, famous all around for their magnificent pools and their almost tangible calm.

And now there's a fish ladder to help them get past the Heïd dam.

2015, leaning over the railing of the bridge above Laroin, watching the fisherman with his graceful, sweeping cast, I notice also a dead fish—a shame, as it's plump and a good 20 inches long—floating, nestled up against the left bank about 30 yards down from where he's standing. I hope he doesn't see it, and I wonder what it died of.

For, despite the fact that the water is brilliantly clear and there's no longer a tannery, a paper mill, a chocolate factory, a wax factory, a soap factory, and countless laundries all using the river's water, it's actually more polluted now than ever, and largely because there are so many more people living along it.

The miracle at Lourdes, about 30 miles upstream, is no small contributor to the problem—six million visitors a year, washing dishes, hands, clothing, flushing toilets, brushing teeth . . .

And though a water treatment plant has been built at Lescar and a major study done in 2012, the cities' sewers still share their canalization with the runoff from the streets and gutters, so whenever there is heavy rainfall or even the slightest flood, all used water all goes directly into the river.

a river is a slippage

                    is its business

                                 river heading elsewhere

with a candle

river longer sideways than its description

                      is its destination

                              flickers because there

always is a wind coming down a river

wavers. and all light wavers with it. a woman walking
along it holding out a lantern. a child walking along it,
jumping from stone to stone to stone
in the dark. someone lights a match
it never reaches.

Lourdes, miraculous and practical: Beginning in the mid-19th century, with the sightings that made it famous, pilgrims lit candles in the grotto and left them there, burning. Their unburned remains would then be thrown into the river, and when the floods came, they would float off with the current and get caught in the shallower, rockier stretches around Pau. The locals would gather them up and melt them down to make new candles. At some point in the 20th century, in response to ecological concerns, a law was passed making it illegal to throw the ends into the river, to the great disappointment of everyone downstream.

river over water

overboard its borders

and all its birds

alder, oak, and poplar

outnumber

the innumerable

snakes, moles, and rabbits

of stone. If you stay

still enough

the wall you build

will sometimes last for

centuries and memory

turn to shelter

that it nonetheless outlives.

There is only one river, and it is in the sun.

Or sunlight stands upon the river

or moves across it like a lathe.

Let's imagine that sunlight could carve it all up

and hold it in its shape.

Or we could say

there is only one sun   and the river within

or the sun, once again, caught again

pouring itself across land.

a river slips

                    in shifting leaves

sifting. a river sifts

                    and falls in pieces

in which not seen

                    (this we never see)

in splices.

                    if fall a great distance, if a river

fall shelter, if a river fall find

several miles slightly off-center.

it took centuries

                    of falling—most rivers

are not actually

                    flowing, but falling

the length of themselves

                    times the sun.

ACKNOWLEDGMENTS

Warmest thanks to the association *Poésie dans les Chais* and its director, Didier Bourda; they generously sponsored two residencies, one in September 2014 and the other in March 2015, during which this text was researched and written. It literally would not exist without them. I'd also like to thank Paul Mirat, whose generosity with information about various aspects of the river and its history, as well as his feedback on the text, was extremely valuable.

Warm thanks also to the editors of the literary reviews *Eleven Eleven*, *The Capilano Review*, and *Plume*, and to the editor of the *Zasterle Anthology*, Manuel Brito, and to that of *The Little American Anthology*, Douglas Messerli, for having published sections of this text, at times in earlier versions.

And a special thanks to Francesca Capone, whose invitation to participate in her project *Writing in Threads* instigated the piece.

COLE SWENSEN (www.coleswensen.com) is the author of fifteen volumes of poetry and a volume of critical essays. She has been a Guggenheim Fellow and a finalist for the National Book Award; her other notations include the Iowa Poetry Prize, the San Francisco State Poetry Center Book Award, a National Poetry Series Selection, and the PEN USA Award in Literary Translation. She is the editor of La Presse (www.lapressepoetry.com) and divides her time between Paris and Providence, RI, where she teaches at Brown University.

GAVE
by Cole Swensen

Cover text set in Century Gothic
Interior text set in Bell Gothic Std, Century Gothic, Garamond 3 Lt Sd

Château d'Henri IV, Pierre Gorse (artist) and Becquet (lithographer)
Bibliothèque Patrimoniale Pau / Médiathèque Andrée Labarrère / cote Ee3213.

Collaged photograph by David Le Deodic

Design & layout by Sharon Zetter

Offset printed in the United States
by Edwards Brothers Malloy, Ann Arbor, Michigan
On 55# Glatfelter B18 Antique
Acid Free Archival Quality Recycled Paper

Publication of this book was made possible in part by gifts from:
The New Place Fund
Robin & Curt Caton

Omnidawn Publishing
Oakland, California
2017

Rusty Morrison & Ken Keegan, senior editors & co-publishers
Gillian Olivia Blythe Hamel, managing editor
Cassandra Smith, poetry editor & book designer
Sharon Zetter, poetry editor, book designer & development officer
Liza Flum, poetry editor & marketing assistant
Peter Burghardt, poetry editor
Juliana Paslay, fiction editor
Gail Aronson, fiction editor
Cameron Stuart, marketing assistant
Avren Keating, administrative assistant
Kevin Peters, *OmniVerse* Lit Scene editor
Sara Burant, *OmniVerse* reviews editor
Josie Gallup, publicity assistant
SD Sumner, copyeditor
Briana Swain, marketing assistant